25 Days
Of Christmas
An Advent Journey

Sharon Vander Meer

CONTENTS

Day 1, Advent – 7
Day 2, Noel, Noel – 8
Day 3, Carols – 9
Day 4, Bells, Bells – 10
Day 5, Christmas – 11
Day 6, Believe – 12
Day 7, Hope – 13
Day 8, Faith – 14
Day 9, Trust – 15
Day 10, Baby Jesus – 16
Day 11, Holy, Holy – 17
Day 12, Son of God – 18
Day 13, Child of Man – 19
Day 14, Worship – 20
Day 15, Joy and Light – 21
Day 16, Immanuel – 22
Day 17, Messiah – 23
Day 18, Angels – 24
Day 19, Shepherd – 25
Day 20, Star of Wonder – 26
Day 21, The Manger – 27
Day 22, Stable – 28
Day 23, Nativity – 29
Day 24, Christ Child – 30
Day 25, Gifts of the Magi – 31

DEDICATION

Robert C. Vander Meer. My husband is kind and loving, supportive and patient. It is through his encouragement I write on.

ACKNOWLEDGMENT

I am blessed to have good friends who responded to my call for beta readers. Everyone I asked, said "yes," and then provided amazing insight. Thank you to these amazing women: Kathy Allen, Carol Linder, Joyce Litherland, Karen Rieniets and Juli Salman. This is a better book because of you.

AN ADVENT JOURNEY

Day 1

Advent

Alleluia!
Dance with joy,
Vow to celebrate
Emmanuel to come,
Now and forever,
The Holy One.

Your thoughts:

And in thy seed shall all the nations of the earth be blessed; because thou hast obeyed my voice. Genesis 22:18

Day 2

Noel, Noel

Newness of hope,
Open your eyes,
Evidence kindness,
Love makes you wise.

Nurture through song,
One story to tell,
Each note of joy,
Lingers – rings like a bell.

Your thoughts:

But thou, Bethlehem Ephratah, though thou be little among the thousands of Judah, yet out of thee shall he come forth unto me that is to be ruler in Israel; whose goings forth have been from of old, from everlasting. Micah 5:2

Day 3

Carols

Call out! Shout for joy!
Advent sings of a baby boy,
Reigning not as a regal king.
One babe in the manger, that's the thing.
Live, love, laugh, dance, sing and shout!
Sharing this, His love, is what Christmas is about.

Your thoughts:

For to us a child is born, to us a son is given, and the government will be on his shoulders. And he will be called Wonderful Counselor, Mighty God, Everlasting Father, Prince of Peace. Isaiah 9:6

Day 4

Bells, Bells

Bells chime sweet songs of joy,
Every note tells of the sweet little boy.
Laughter lights my heart this day.
Listen! Hear it? Bells ring, He's on His way.
Sing bells, ring bells, chime His story and His glory.

Bells chime peace to you and me
Engaging hope and faith so we can see,
Lights of promise pave the road with gold,
Lilting music melodies of happiness unfold.
Sing bells, ring bells, chime His story and His glory.

Your thoughts:

Behold, the days come, saith the LORD, that I will raise unto David a righteous Branch, and a King shall reign and prosper, and shall execute judgment and justice in the earth. Jeremiah 23:5

Day 5

Christmas

Christ the King, of Him we sing,
Hark! He comes, let music ring!
Reverberate this glorious sound,
Inspiring all, let joy abound.
Sing the melody of love
Trust and faith from God above.
Merry all who sing His grace,
Angel heralds bless this holy place.
Serenity and peace let us embrace.

Your thoughts:

And the spirit of the LORD shall rest upon him, the spirit of wisdom and understanding, the spirit of counsel and might, the spirit of knowledge and of the fear of the Lord. Isaiah 11:2

11

Day 6

Believe

Because we are watched over in all ways,
Emmanuel floods hope through our days,
Lasting love sets hearts ablaze.
Infinite praise of His miraculous birth,
Evidence of God, come down to earth,
Victory over despair, death and sin,
Enriched when through Christ, He let us in.

Your thoughts:

Of the increase of his government and peace there shall be no end, upon the throne of David, and upon his kingdom, to order it, and to establish it with judgment and with justice from henceforth even for ever. The zeal of the LORD of hosts will perform this. Isaiah 9:7

Day 7

Hope

Hope and happiness,
Opportunity and trust,
Promised His presence,
Encounter our Lord, He is just.

Your thoughts:

And God said unto Abraham, Let it not be grievous in thy sight because of the lad, and because of thy bondwoman; in all that Sarah hath said unto thee, hearken unto her voice; for in Isaac shall thy seed be called. Genesis 21:12

Day 8

Faith

Friend to all, enemy of none,
Angels would guard Him for he is the One.
Incited, indicted, some would shun
Thinking to deny Him, He would be done.
He overcame all, because of Him *we* have won.

Your thoughts:

Your throne, O God, will last for ever and ever; a scepter of justice will be the scepter of your kingdom. You love righteousness and hate wickedness; therefore God, your God, has set you above your companions by anointing you with the oil of joy. Psalm 45:6-7

Day 9

Trust

Truth, the word feared most of all.
Rhetoric and lies, cause us to fall.
Utmost and highest, we aspire to call,
Savior sweet Savior, ere death's bitter gall!
Trust I give you, my life, my all.

Your thoughts:

The scepter will not depart from Judah, nor the ruler's staff from between his feet, until he to whom it belongs shall come and the obedience of the nations shall be his. Genesis 49:10

Day 10

Baby Jesus

Behold he comes in quiet grace
A child so small, fair of face.
Believe this gift of love is for all
You, me, and each who hears the call.

Justice in His every lesson,
Each a message, and a blessing.
Son of God, what does He say?
Ushering hope and faith each day,
Sacred yet human, He comes this way.

Your thoughts:

When Israel was a child, then I loved him, and called my son out of Egypt. Hosea 11:1

Day 11

Holy, Holy

Heralds sing
Of the King.
Let voices ring.
Yule love He does bring.

Heaven sing,
Our newborn king,
Lovely angel Noels ring,
Yes, new Light He does bring.

Your thoughts:

The voice of him that crieth in the wilderness, Prepare ye the way of the LORD, make straight in the desert a highway for our God. Isaiah 40:3

Day 12

Son of God

Spirit of God, Holy Father of all,
Over and in us, lest we fall,
Now come sweet Jesus, heed our call.

Open to any who seek relief
Faithful and trusting, filled with belief.

God the Father come down to earth,
Omniscient and holy seeing mankind's worth,
Devine, yet human in His lowly birth.

Your thoughts:

Every valley shall be exalted, and every mountain and hill shall be made low: and the crooked shall be made straight, and the rough places plain: Isaiah 40:4

Day 13

Child of Man

Chosen by God
Humble Mary,
In trust you said, 'yes.'
Leaning on faith,
Dedicated to serve.
Offering your body to be
Filled with the hope of all.
Mother Mary, courageous one,
Appointed by God to bring
New life to all the world.

Your thoughts:

And the glory of the Lord shall be revealed, and all flesh shall see it together: for the mouth of the Lord hath spoken it. Isaiah 40:5

Day 14

Worship

Wonder of wonders, the shepherds in awe
Open and worshipful as angels they saw.
Rise up, go to Bethlehem and see Him there,
Sleeping in a manger, there were no rooms to spare.
He sleeps, He is human, He is but a child,
In the loving arms of parents so mild.
Praise Him, through Him we are reconciled.

Your thoughts:

He is despised and rejected of men; a man of sorrows, and acquainted with grief: and we hid as it were our faces from him; he was despised, and we esteemed him not. Isaiah 53:3

Day 15

Joy and Light

Joyful sounds, Angel voices say,
Obedient to God, He will pray,
Yes, His life will light the way.

Amazing gift of grace He will be,
New light He will bring to you and me,
Devine yet human by God's decree.

Life giving hope He does bestow
Inspiring trust, Him we know,
Goodness shared helps us grow.
He lived to teach so we may show
Thanks to God as in light we go.

Your thoughts:

And thou Bethlehem, in the land of Judah, art not the least among the princes of Juda: for out of thee shall come a Governor, that shall rule my people Israel. Matthew 2:6

21

Day 16

Immanuel

Immanuel, Christ the Lord
Most high and above all.
Majestic
And
Nobel? Not at all.
Unique, yes, but humble of birth
Embracing humanity in His manger
Lighting the way giving life to hope.

Your thoughts:

The LORD thy God will raise up unto thee a Prophet from the midst of thee, of thy brethren, like unto me; unto him ye shall hearken.
Deuteronomy 18:15

Day 17

Messiah

Make way for the Lord, He has come
Emmanuel, God with us, for everyone.
Sacred and Holy, yet present each day.
Soul-filling and faithful, to Him we pray.
Inspiring, blessing, peace-giving and pure,
Abiding in love, of Him we are sure,
His peace will come, and ever endure.

Your thoughts:

And there shall come forth a rod out of the stem of Jesse, and a Branch shall grow out of his roots. Isaiah 11:1

Day 18

Angels

Angels shout, their voices ring,
Nobel and watchful, awaiting the king.
Glorify God! they cry in the night,
Extraordinary! The gift of Grace comes in Light.
Let all humankind embrace this babe so mild,
Sleeping in a manger here, He is the Christ Child.

Your thoughts:

The people that walked in darkness have seen a great light: they that dwell in the land of the shadow of death, upon them hath the light shined. Isaiah 9:2

Day 19

Shepherd

Shepherd tending your flock by night.
Heralds appear, what a sight!
Extolling a king asleep in a place so plain,
Portent of the gift humankind will gain.
Hurry, see him, this babe small and dear,
Emblem of hope, no need to fear.
Radiant vision? No, only an infant so mild,
Devine yet humbly born, this wee little child.

Your thoughts:

And there were in the same country shepherds abiding in the field, keeping watch over their flock by night. Luke 2:8

Day 20

Star of Wonder

Stars are celestial guides
Transforming the night sky into
A map to places longed for but unknown,
Radiating light so travelers may find their way.
One travels this track in the belly of a maid,
Father Joseph leading the beast of burden
Wending its way to Bethlehem.
Others follow a special star, searching for a king –
Not a child, not a babe in the arms of a tired woman.
Didn't they hear there would be a king? And yet
Each magi kneels and gives gifts to this child,
Recognizing the man he would become, wise and wondrous.

Your thoughts:

He shall be great, and shall be called the Son of the Highest: and the Lord God shall give unto him the throne of his father David: And he shall reign over the house of Jacob forever; and of his kingdom there shall be no end. Luke 1:32-33

Day 21

The Manger

There he lay in a trough where animals took food.
His place of rest could hardly be described as the best,
Emptied for use as a crib for this inexplicable little babe.
Merciful and mighty? You would never know it.
And why should you? He is born in a stable
Not in the gilded halls of a queen with midwives in attendance.
God came to earth as human as anyone, a child
Endearing to those who claimed him as their own, and yet
Radiating power, bringing kings and shepherds to their knees.

Your thoughts:

And she brought forth her firstborn son, and wrapped him in swaddling clothes, and laid him in a manger; because there was no room for them in the inn. Luke 2:7

Day 22

Stable

Son of God, child of man,
To each of us you sing a singular song,
Anthems to touch the hearts of all.
Believers and questioners,
Lost souls seeking peace and hope,
Each looking to the Light streaming from a stable.

Your thoughts:

And this shall be a sign unto you; Ye shall find the babe wrapped in swaddling clothes, lying in a manger. Luke 2:12

Day 23

Nativity

Noel, noel, breaks the silence of the night,
Angel voices proclaim to all,
This One comes to bring new light
Into the hearts of those who hear His call.
Validating the promises of old,
Into this world would come a child
To bring change and newness to every soul.
Yes, because of Him we are reconciled.

Your thoughts:

And it came to pass, as the angels were gone away from them into heaven, the shepherds said one to another, Let us now go even unto Bethlehem, and see this thing which is come to pass, which the Lord hath made known unto us. Luke 2:15

Day 24

Christ Child

Christmas bells ring and chime,
Heralding news, happy and sublime.
Resonating with sounds transcendent,
Inspiring hope and joy, magnificent.
Sing we now with heaven's angel throng
This happy news in heartfelt song.
Comes He now, a wee infant heart,
Hearing, seeing, breathing, life to impart.
Immanuel, God with us now and forever,
Leading us to live, laugh, and endeavor,
Declaring faith and joy at the birth of this baby boy.

Your thoughts:

And they came with haste, and found Mary, and Joseph, and the babe lying in a manger. And when they had seen it, they made known abroad the saying which was told them concerning this child. Luke 2:16-17

Day 25

Gifts of the Magi

God's great gift
Inspired newness of life,
Faith-centered, driven by trust.
Trust sparking compassion,
Service, mercy, kindness, and empathy.
One act of goodness
Fosters another and another,
Telling of courage and generosity, and of
Hope for a better world – created
Each day – good deed by good deed.
Magi brought gifts fit for a king
And practical in the way of the time,
Gifts that could be used and shared,
Inspiring all to do the same with gifts given to us.

Your thoughts:

And when they were come into the house, they saw the young child with Mary his mother, and fell down, and worshipped him: and when they had opened their treasures, they presented unto him gifts; gold, and frankincense and myrrh. Matthew 2:11

ABOUT THE AUTHOR

Sharon Vander Meer has spent much of her career as a freelance writer, reporter and editor. She has been a storyteller since childhood and finds inspiration in everyday life. In addition to *25 Days of Christmas, An Advent Journey*, she has written three novels: *Finding Family, Future Imperfect* and the *Ballad of Bawdy McClure* (available in e-format as *Thunder Prime, Fog Island*). She has also written a book of inspirational readings, *Not Just Another Day*. Her books are available at amazon.com and by contacting her directly at fsharon@msn.com.

Sharon lives in the beautiful northern mountains of New Mexico in the original Las Vegas, which has a history dating back to 1835. She is married and is a mom and grandmother.

www.ingramcontent.com/pod-product-compliance
Lightning Source LLC
Chambersburg PA
CBHW071803020426
42331CB00008B/2397